EMERALD

BY THE SAME AUTHOR

POETRY
Alibi
Summer Snow
Angel
Fusewire
Rembrandt Would Have Loved You
Voodoo Shop
The Soho Leopard
Darwin: A Life in Poems
The Mara Crossing
Learning to Make an Oud in Nazareth
Tidings: A Christmas Journey

FICTION
Where the Serpent Lives

NON-FICTION
In and Out of the Mind: Greek Images of the Tragic Self
Whom Gods Destroy: Elements of Greek and Tragic Madness
I'm a Man: Sex, Gods and Rock 'n' Roll
Tigers in Red Weather
52 Ways of Looking at a Poem
The Poem and the Journey
Silent Letters of the Alphabet

EDITING
Walter Ralegh: Selected Poems
*Alfred Lord Tennyson: Poems with Introduction
    and Notes*
Gerard Manley Hopkins: Poems

EMERALD

Ruth Padel

Chatto & Windus
LONDON

1 3 5 7 9 10 8 6 4 2

Chatto & Windus, an imprint of Vintage,
20 Vauxhall Bridge Road,
London SW1V 2SA

Chatto & Windus is part of the Penguin Random House
group of companies whose addresses can be found at
global.penguinrandomhouse.com

Copyright © Ruth Padel 2018

First published by Chatto & Windus in 2018

penguin.co.uk/vintage

A CIP catalogue record for this book is
available from the British Library

ISBN 9781784741075

Typeset in 11/14 pt Minion Pro
by Integra Software Services Pvt Ltd, Pondicherry

Printed and bound by Clays Ltd, St Ives plc

Penguin Random House is committed to a sustainable future
for our business, our readers and our planet. This book is made
from Forest Stewardship Council® certified paper.

In memory of Hilda Padel

1919–2017

'Green is a solace,
a promise of peace, a fort
against the cold'

—William Carlos Williams

Contents

EMERALD

The Emerald Tablet

This is to do with being lost
    with believing that the truth
is buried in some special place
    difficult to find

and a hero of ancient wisdom
    Moses   Borges   Gandalf
that stern but kind
    oracle-giving grandfather you never had

will pop out of the green
    out of the woodwork   to reveal it

encrypted on a slab of emerald
    by the king of a forgotten world
in exquisite bas-relief lettering
    similar to the earliest Phoenician script.

It will contain formulae for an antique magic
    going back to early Egypt
transparent in our world as a flame in daylight
    but still with power to burn

and will tell you that what is inward
    buried in earth   in flesh   and in your mind
is also the bright surface of the world outside
    and is divine.

It will start by saying above is the same as below
meaning   I think   our loneliness is not alone

and will go on to say that spirit
    does not   as we have been told
keep trying to peel away from atoms of your body
    but is embedded in nature

and you   yourself   are the crucible
in which base metal can be turned to gold.

    *

This is to do with transformation
   with the dead
     and where they are inside you
once they are gone.

Above is the same as below.
I have set up a headshot of my mum
    by the kettle in a wooden frame.
I meet her eyes

in the half-light as I make coffee
   and keep her with me
as I trickle down the black iron nerve
of a station I don't understand.

      I have lost my mobile phone
      with its mysteriously living map

      the blue pulsar of identity has disappeared
      and the cross-over

on my little foldout guide
is scuffed   torn

unreadable
exactly where I was hoping to go.

　　*

Where do you start　　faced with the shadow
　　of these half-moon globes　　on their slender
　　　pistachio columns　　marking descent to the subway
to recover that pealing of bells
　　you'd taken for granted
when someone who really knows you　　gets it?

One sleepless night after the funeral
I saw for sale on the net
an *Emerald Tablet Key-Ring* made in Seville
　　a resin replica
of what it might have looked like　　verified
by the International Guild of Alchemists.

I sent off for one　　but the resin feels
like soapy biscuit and the mystic marks
mean nothing. Who knows what it looked like anyway?
All we have　　all we ever have　　are words.
　　They say Balinas the Wise
discovered it thirteen hundred years ago

he entered a cave in Sri Lanka　　found
a statue of Hermes　　god of dreams　　climbed down
to a vault beneath　　saw an old man sitting on a throne
cradling a tablet glowing in the dark like crème de menthe
　　mistletoe on a winter branch
and recorded what it said　　in Arabic.

Jung saw it too   in his dream
     of the unconscious as a shimmering
table of green stone
     at which he sat alone   in an Italian loggia
above white rocks and a sapphire lagoon
     that giddy sunlit place   where we all

might feel in touch with what is deepest in us
longing as we do   for the adept
who will see our truth and not be appalled
     who will transform
the writing in our own cave
to a magic formula   for us to live by   now.

We are all trying   in our way   to understand
secrets of nature   secrets of the soul.
Why are we talking of the end of the world?

     *

We've met as arranged   in the glass hall
                                        of a library full of light
and talk of the lure of hidden knowledge.
Over salad and linguini
all the animals of the wilderness
the shy white helleborine orchid
and the hidden paths
               to and from the cedar forest
mourn   with the backward grace
of a cry from the broken-open heart
for all our mothers.

     *

This is your journey   no one else's.
Your passage through love
        friendship   grief
is and will go on being a perpetual process.

Touch the threshold
from days of your childhood.
Climb the worn stairway
to the terrace of York stone
patched with rosemary *tortuosa* and blue thyme.

Walk the parapet   your hair blowing in the wind
    and study the foundations
        laid by the Seven Sages
                        remember?
Enter the temple   the sanctum
    unveil the box
    unlatch the bronze lock
    untie the silk cord
        above the hidden opening
and take out a tablet of emerald
that tells of trials you endured.

The flowering orchards
and towering ziggurat say
    This is you.
This is what you have made
of yourself so far.
You quested to boundaries of earth
for the meaning of life
and found it in your own backyard.

The tablet says you will emerge
in a magical garden by the sea
and enter the tavern of loss
which is also the moment of truth.

Astray

The wound is where the light gets in
but what is light? When your mother
dies   you lose other things too
your sense of direction

like faceting a jewel
     cutting away precious mineral
to let the rays go deeper   farther
     make the orphan gem
more valuable
     turn the crystal to the fire.

Life   said Joseph Conrad
is a midnight ride
over barely cooled lava
you might fall through the crust any minute.

Nursing Wing

Where have you escaped to
   still air of the nursing wing
   last room on the corridor
we shared in those long   hushed   hours

air breathed by a dying mother
with all her children round her
as she goes
       labouring
             towards the light
climbing new Himalayas at every breath
  resolute   as always
  glasses off but unafraid.

Forgive me   little-wing   for opening a window
    when we filled her hands
    with snowdrops and myrtle
to let her spirit out
    losing you in compound shiftings of the breeze
      ruffling the blackbird   standing guard
      over February buds
      on the bare cherry tree outside.

I have heard your molecules   stir
somewhere else since
some place I cannot remember
and when I stepped out into the cold whisper of March
you had gone

        gentle
        dust-filled
        exact

your particles of time
        your frost damage
        and mystery pentangles
        of family relationships
lifting
into the smoke of ordinary life
like starlings spiralling to roost
in the Avalon Marshes

where last November
a white egret waited
        hunched   alone
in half-ignited sunset
angling for eels
in the bountiful waters of Ham Wall
        until the first mist
of incomers danced across the heavens

and a million birds
        which close up   we knew   would be shimmering
            with metallic oils
        sapphire   emerald   violet
            pointilliste   on charcoal feathers

spun
    into a shape-shifter silhouette
balled up tight as a balloon
     then loosening
         to soot chiffon
             stretching across white sky

a nursing wing
with the helical twist of DNA
and folded swirl of a tornado.
First time in all her ninety-seven years
   she witnessed
         a murmuration.

Clast

When your mother dies
there's no one left to hold the sky.
   When I was small
we lived on the top floor
in Wimpole Street   an attic window
looking out on a forest canopy of silver tiles
   where an owl
roosted in a revolving flue
after a long night's hunting in Hyde Park.
   When the wind blew
my mother held me up to see the vent
   swinging its cowl
   like a periscope
and two dark eyes appeared
looking back at us
from a nimbus of pale feathers.
   Face of a secret moon.

  *

In the last week
when we were all
        cancelling meetings
        making long-distance phone calls wherever we could find a signal
        gathering over scratch meals
        running out of milk

that moment when true feelings light up suddenly
out of the square-cut stone of the everyday
and urgency swings in like a wrecking ball

one of my brothers told us
that her twenty-first birthday   fell
during the London blitz.

Rainy September.
   Her brothers all away
                   working in hospitals
                                submarines
                                   labs in America

she was alone   with her disabled
older sister and their parents.
None of them remembered   until supper
                                when her mother
                                went upstairs
and came back with a ring.

I don't like to think of this.
No one excited for her
   as her brothers might have been
only something quick-found   that would do

in the blackout   autumn rain
            twenty miles from fires
      shaking   thunder on the night horizon.

That ring
      a piece of stuck-together love and hurt
splintered   by the invading shale or schist
                                of loneliness

I never heard of it till now
never saw it on her finger. Will we find it
in the small bashed-up brown case

of jewellery she never wore
that we lugged to those valuers
for probate

or was it got rid of   lost
    given away
through the years that came after?

How do you prove
    and what can you value
under the mountain range

of the unconscious?
    We never ask
the bedrock question till too late.

The Crystallization of Tears

I captured the first tear
rolling down my cheek
with a micro pipette

dispensed it into small drops on a slide
and tried standard light techniques
    bright field   polarize.

Both were beautiful
    with something missing. I installed
dark field on my microscope.

On a background black as outer space
my tear lit up like a little planet
a perfect silver circle

whose inner crystal
    garden   glowed
like the random parquetry of frost.

Everyone   some moment in their life
will need *dark field*
to recognize the peculiar shapes of their own tear

each tiny   whisper-white
webbed circuit
of bladed needles   is unique

and tears of emotion   O light
are different again.
Let them fall.

Every split-second crying   you create
new Milky Ways of micro-filigree
new mineral swirls   of splinter flakes

glyco-proteins
    binding with mucins   packed in a snow globe
not one structure repeated.

> *Tears of sorrow   tears of laughter*
> *tears to protect the eye from blowing dust.*
> *Tears at onion irritation*
> *tears from your left eye and right*
> *tears shed when the final barrier*
>   *has just*
>   *gone down*

> *tears for all your broken ties*
> *tears from every unlit town*
> *fury   happiness   disaster*
> *and somewhere at the last*
>   *diastole in the cycle of the heart*
> *tears of consolation.*

Here's to goodbye. Here's to the tears
I knew I'd cry. She'd have loved
how each fresh-minted sphere

crystallizes as it dries
in its own one-off design. Tomorrow
I'm going to x-ray every drop and find out why.

◆

A Trip to the Moon

Our mother is moving house.
She's ninety-one
and determined. She wants to go
she says   to where she can die.

Words like *sheltered accommodation*
are coming at us from outer space
but it's not like that   not yet

there will be spare rooms
in the new place   a garden
she can feed nuthatches
cook her own food. Still

down the hill will be a sanatorium
a clinic   an Alzheimer's wing.
She doesn't want *to be a burden.*

In every corner a vermillion string
to pull if she falls. I clear
the cupboards   pass over secret histories
in every blanket's stain and burn.

Should she sell the oversize kitchen clock
she still climbs a stepladder
on Sunday to wind

to the blind piano-tuner
who took a shine to it

when he came to value
the piano that's never played

or should it wait
for some grandchild to give it a home?
For the first time in her life

she'll live with things only she
has chosen. No husband or children to consider
no furniture from aunts.
She can sell things. Give them away.

Traumas of today   contracts to exchange
dates of completion   arguments
over who will let the carpenter in

to measure up in her new home
will be forgotten. Because   let's face it
    forgetting's the issue.
And she is facing it. She knows

that from now on   three
    miles from family
she's in an unknown zone.

Removal Men

All day I watch our lives go into the van.
When my brother has got my mother away with the plants
they carry out the kitchen table   armchairs
and the mad bronze over-size speakers

sixty years of listening to *Carols from Kings*
in a hot kitchen on Christmas Eve.
I unscrew the letter casket
flanking the front door

and spend an hour untwining a nest-box
last employed by blue tits
from a lace-cap hydrangea
and the wilderness of wire she twisted beneath.

I set up my stall like Canute
at the folding table we picnicked on
when we were small   and see the gold Chinese horseman
on the front of the grandfather clock   disappear

along with the great black bookcase
the sofa   seven beds   the standard lamp
till I'm on my own with an empty house
and look down from her bedroom

on the garden they made together
white rowan   lacebark pine   and the little apple tree
    part-collapsed under climbing grandchildren
overgrown by a flowering creeper.

I remove her low-energy bulb
the upside-down lampshade
   and look at the space
where the bed stood   where my father died.

That furred rasp in his throat. Liquid morphine
when breathing grew difficult. Little sips
     hour after hour
then all breath finally stopped

and the buyer of Roman glass
the cellist   lover of Homer and Horace
the painter of new theories of object relations
on dodecahedrons   was gone.

Part-Arc of a Rainbow

As if you saw

    driving back from a sprint to the supermarket
    to get your nearly   but not quite   dying mum
    a pack of squeegee sponges and a new
    washing-up brush   the old one is filthy
    she can hardly see the sink any more

something you've never come across before

    the part-arc of a rainbow
    slicing through a chink in metal cloud

and as you go

    that stump of rainbow fades
    but shreds of its hidden core   appear
      in other sectors of grey air
    like swamp-light   flashing out of
    and back into   the corner of your eye

as if somewhere beyond all this heaviness

    there's a whole skyful of neon
    some wild fishnet pyre
    of the spectrum   all the glittering hidden
    wavelengths of memory   tangled as the ancient cottons
    in her long-abandoned sewing-casket

it is a rainbow strip-tease

you will never see the end
and because you're on a curly country road
the angles keep shifting   you don't know
who or what is round the next bend
until you see the whole semi-circumference entire.

She Liked a Laugh

She hated pink   hydrangeas   marzipan
woolly thinking and pretence.
She stuck to tap-water
   wouldn't have any truck
with Perrier   superstition   bling.

She believed in hard fact
               how and why
                    the daily crossword
                             jokes
                Latin names of plants
          comedy TV
     and going on

when eyes and ears
and muscles failed   setting her alarm
for eight a.m.
    even when the last
nerve-ends in her fingers withered
so she took an hour   alone
   refusing help
to do up zips and buttons.

What if I'd said   one evening
lighting the lamp   cooking dinner
while she took in the weather forecast

I believe

that emeralds   come
from planet Venus
are found in nests of griffins
emit the energy of Saturn
reveal the truth
when placed under the tongue
and their powers are spiritual
balance   wisdom   love
the re-awakening of spring?

I can just see
                    the grin.
Oh *Ruth*!

Your Life as a Wave

*'Inside any old person is a young person wondering
what happened.'* — TERRY PRATCHETT

Born in the main of light
lily-fire on the horizon
you become a spirit of the water
governed by the moon
luminous as the veil of the Medusa.

You dance through spray
like blossom from a pear tree
floating free   as the soprano
of Victoria de los Angeles
in *Songs of the Auvergne.*

Then storms send you haywire.
Time   which used to be your friend
catches up with you.
What with the artificial elbow
shoulder pain   lost words and memories

Time rushes   Time becomes a roar
of ocean currents   and you lose yourself
in sliding foam on the pebbled shore.
But what if you were born
here   where the tide comes in

with seeds of what you may become
concealed in bladder-wrack
like the carbon star in a trapiche emerald?
The ripple-lace of surf
that's where the wave begins.

Fonteyn   not as the Dying Swan
but bright Undine. Suppose we move
towards uncharted beauty. Age
means no more living on a knife-edge
but a pure delight

in slatted shadows on the wall
the sunlit garden   sudden flight
of goldfinches. You gaze out at the night
and see a square of yellow
where there was   or used to be

no house. Want to re-find
who you were? You never can.
There's only *on*.
Away from the pebbled shore
to the main of light.

Appraisal

I liked that   said my mum.
Makes it all sound
not quite so bad. Read it again.
What's the main of light?

Quantum Linked

She was so sure there's nothing beyond.
No sign-bearer
running through interstellar fields
could have tempted her to say

When I die   I'll see the lining of the world
the other side   beyond the hearing aids
*   the sycamore seedlings   cracked pelvis*
and the awful forgetting.

No gods. No omens.
But in the land of the setting sun
we are hungry for fruits of the real
and what she believed in was the bond

of entangled photons
    smallest light particles
    quantum linked   however far away
between children   family   the earth.

Imago

    determines the way you apprehend others
the long-ago star-flicker of a soul
                 as it crystallized
based on your earliest relations
fantasized or real   with your family
as with a sacred oak   or the black velvet of Tashkent

another person's early imprint on your heart
blazoning the forest floor
   shadow of their presence
   path of their tornado
burnt into you like poker-work.

Take the hidden
      holy medal
           of   let's say   a father's image.

The colours of other men
      I encounter on my way through life
will provoke an underhand return
         some re-melt or re-issue
of that deep-iron-cast relationship.

Imago   the original first cell   always there but rarely seen
in thrall to the drunk coachman of repression
translating stony idioms of the underworld
     to neurons in the brain

always ready to pop up unbidden
     triggered for instance by a mother's death

will rule how I respond
      to lilacs in the rain
      quiet of the desert
      lullaby of bird-land
      spark of the arrow's flight
      the silken lips
           of blond
      jackal-headed gods in a midnight city
      and interlacing leaves of paradise
                    today.

Here they are   the old monsters.
Bones moving through mist.

Green Flash

That emerald ray   which my father
showed me over the mountains
a small electric bud like a Smartie

green   always my favourite
     frozen pea
on the scarlet arc of a plunging sun

something only ever seen from far away
when the horizon is clear   as it never is in real life
              no danger of contact

for one split second   you might spot
the final eyebrow
of the sun   change colour

because   you know Ruth   when the chromosphere
begins to dip into the horizon
colours of the spectrum disappear.

The atmosphere refracts light
like a prism   bends the rays
separates the colours   they go down alone

one at a time
     like children
following a piper into a hill

with the eldest   red
     the longest wave-length
     on its velvet rope   the first to go.

It requires a well-layered atmosphere
and a good relationship with the air
                          the world
                          each other

to let the index of refraction properly increase
as in the wild green dragon flames
of Aurora Borealis.

When all the sun's disc is above the horizon
    and the soul
is scrambling along in its ordinary way

through day's light-saturated provision of the mind
the colours overlap
you can't see them on their own

but in dying light   as the sun declines
   into the mountains   into a clear sea
   and slides   or appears to slide   down
   under the horizon

something on its shoulder seems
    if you're in the right place
    if you're with the right person
to flash   like the *Go* of a traffic signal green.

Blink and you'll miss it
    that one brief glow
    of understanding
never truly found.

Second Chance

Last night he landed in our kitchen.
A dream   of course
   but when did I ever dream
of him doing anything
but judging and turning away

now here he was   after she died
      no Erl King or Scythian marauder
just ordinary   gentle
asking for a cup of tea. He had been ill
and came among us in her turquoise dressing-gown.

Is it the world that's changed
      or something in my mind?
I touched his shoulder and a bird flew in
up to the rafters   twittering
      blundering

a swallow   someone said
and opened a window. It spun off safe
      into blue air
reminding me of that ache
you feel   when a wound from long ago

opens up like a second chance
to lay your finger on
      the calyx   omphalos   eye of the storm
whatever you   cards on the table   valued all along
and never knew.

Iridescent

In autumn   said the potter
on Lang-Po mountain
looking at the slopes after firing

porcelain shapes   green as these hills
appear from the kiln
like snakes after shedding their skin.

But when the storm has passed
    said Emperor Shi-Zong   blue sky
shines through breaks in the cloud.

The potter walked away and made a miracle
porcelain no one has ever seen
    except Shi-Zong

because *Secret* means *Reserved for Royalty*
    and this   you can bet
was beauty that only royalty could wish into being

a two-way
        photonic   dance

of the spectrum
    a thin-film half-light colour

depending on who was looking
    yet there was only the Emperor

dream-blue
    or was it green

fragile as breath
bright as a mirror
resonant as a musical stone.

A musical stone. Wouldn't that be a miracle too?

Fragile as Breath

I give you *Soft Phonation*
    Absolute Jitter
        *Turbulence of the Vocal Fold*s

yellow and red cross-noggins
        shooting in all directions
            from white space

record of a magnifying glass
    laid over my tongue
      and twin electrodes

over the larynx
      measuring cliffs of fall
        as I slur an octave

my voice
    on computer printout
        in the Ear Nose and Throat Hospital

and here come the instructions.
    Breathe deeper   quicker   flex
        the mulberry pearl

of uvula and epiglottis
    the double mollusc of your vocal cords
        quivering before the pharyngeal arch.

Squeeze from the belly.
   Your muscles should be fast
      as trampolines.

Your voice is your breath.
    The first thing that's yours
                and the last.

Tuning Your Lyre Among the Shades

Blown
    like soot
        through a chink
            in the window-frame

I'm entering a stone world
the Porto Arturo shaft
   through Security
to the charcoal frogmouth
bowels of the mine
wearing waterproofs
a saffron-glaze hard hat
rubber boots and gloves.

The iron cup
      of a platform-cage
winches me down the dark
         through rushing floods.

Forty metres. Can I trust the chain?
   I don't belong
here   nothing human possibly could.
Forty more. The water's warm
   the motor rattles
   the temperature rises
hot enough to suffocate
Orpheus in his song.

Carbon Labyrinth

If you are looking for love
try the mysteries of earth

    splash and crouch through running water
    the pitch-black sauna

        honeycomb of tunnels   molten as a cauldron
        haunted by a dream

            of flashing absinthe
            and the serpent-scales of Melusine.

Now you're blind

   here's torchlight
   a hundred black-smeared faces

now you're deaf

   a hundred claw-point grabbers
   scratch and tease the roof.

A call comes   *Here*!
and everyone stampedes.

A thousand jackhammers
        ten thousand ricochets

                from a seam
                    of dazzle-green

apple frost
    inside black stone

mineral moss
    blossoming in the dark

capillaries of rock
    like unripe sugar crust

a marsh-light whisper
    of fantasies embedded in the bone.

Each swing of the pick
might make your fortune.

Oxygen levels plummet
no one cares

  for this might prove
    the final rising into light

    an opened zip
      the finally answered prayer.

Above is the Same as Below

A shock
that the sky's still here
like uncollected letters.

This slow   new   sunrise
feathers emerald slopes
of cloud-forest and sugar cane

with slanting rose. A flock
of teenage girls
carbon faces   carbon all

over their once-bright dresses
carbon hands and carbon arms
they trawl abandoned shafts

and their mothers
shoulder-deep in river   poke
through rushing shallows

for a glimpse of the enchanter
wild eyes   wet clothes   a panda blur
of blackened faces

that's all of us
sifting the dark
in our anonymities   and hope.

◆

Intermission

She stabilized. She started dying
and then stopped. My brother said
her aneurysm had sealed   stuck

between a kidney and her spine
with no place for blood to leak.
I'm on the way out

she kept saying to friends and family
daring them to say she wasn't.
Perky   almost belligerent.

    It was always hard for her to feel valued.
    Her combative talk
    was more loving than sugary words.

She was surprised
how many people wanted to speak to her   say goodbye
see her one more time   weak as she was

people who never cried
weeping on the phone
she cheered up visitors with gossip

    tell me   how many men
    did your mother
    sleep with   really? I've always wondered.

I held my mobile to her ear
so she could chat
with my daughter in Colombia

a grandson in Barcelona
another in Palestine
and her sister-in-law

in a bad way too
who said in her soft voice
I shall follow you soon.

Jaipur

I can't go to India
    I said   with you in this state
don't be silly.
How can I go to Rajasthan
                through fog-bound Delhi
                a six-hour change of plane
with an exploding aneurysm
hanging like the sword of Damocles in your back?

She argued   insisted   she would be ok
and sent me off   but how did I know
    I'd see her again
    in the chaotic traffic of Jaipur
    taxis on strike
taking an auto-rickshaw to the Old Bazaar
    pink-walled alleys
        colour of embers in a fading sky
    filling up with motorbikes
    electric cables   open drawers
    of secondhand CDs
    a hanging alphabet of Export Surplus shirts
and Rhesus macaques
running over red-tiled roofs in rubber masks?

By the postern to the emerald dealer's yard
a baby monkey   slid
    down a lamp-post like a fireman
    dashed across the street
she'd have cheered him on

the cutter   in his tucked-away white desk
    with a fluoride swing-light
        emeralds   he said   are all about light
had a milky eye like a moonstone
    something wrong since birth

he took linen pouches of raw gems
out of hidden panels in the wall
and poured them in my hand
    while the dealer told the jewel story of his town
owners   brokers   the old Jain trading castes
and emerald cutters
        most of them Muslim
        for hope can be found the other side of pain
        green is the colour of Paradise
        and for five hundred years
        the Mughal emperors
        ordered enormous crystals up from obscure shafts
            beneath the carbon heart
        of Andes. Pink City
        became Emerald City   adept
        in the unique cutting properties of emerald
the only stone in which the flaws are prized.

She was right of course. Still here
when I got back   to northern winter
early snowdrops   steel-wool skies
the sun invisible   burning somewhere else   Jaipur
        and everyone anxious
                        shaky as a bubble
                                in a carpenter's level.
Signs taken for wonders. One hand upon the door.

Logbook

The little daily shock
that she is not
still   flicking her fins
in the solitary kitchen.

Postern

Anything can snag unexpectedly
like this photo of an empty doorway
   framed by splitting lattice
   and a half-panel
   of weather-hammered oak
wedged open to let us in   or out.

Dead leaves   like years   blow
across the floor
where we must be standing   looking through
   to grey-gold mist on rolling hills
where she would feel at home.

You can almost smell
   the creosote   boot dust   crumbled twine
   and rotting deck-chairs
turning   like us all
to junk and rust.

What am I thinking of? The abandoned summerhouse
   below and out of sight
   of the upper lawn
in the garden where she grew up.
This is my mind   telling me
that's where she's gone.

Gorey Bay, Jersey, 1933

In sepia
    sun bonnet
    bleached
    tartan shorts
standing in a wet Vesuvius
of rilling sea and sand

she's an explorer
    at the summit of a mountain
leaning on a knobbled spade.

She did tell me she went to Jersey once
saw cabbages so huge
that the villagers
    like mythical inhabitants on a medieval map
    at the edge of the known world
used the stalks for walking sticks.

She's a chorus girl
    putting forward a long bare leg
with the tide coming in all round her
a flood of lapping glass
    set to wreck
that sandcastle any minute.

She is fourteen   her face in shadow
    gazing   smiling
at someone along the beach.

Yes   when your mother dies you lose the key
    to so many neural pathways
    you had it in your hand
    and now will never know
where it fits the *Mappa Mundi*
of her life

but when   last year
I found this photo in a box under the bed
she said   *Nice legs. Wish I'd had legs like that.*
    You did. That's you!
She didn't believe it   and I can't believe
she isn't here   to show her this again.

Burning the Chaff

One hazard I didn't expect   how you long
to stay where you were   not move on
from who you were   when she was around
to hold you in her unburnt mind   and laugh.

You want to keep the pain alight
as on a summer evening a little grid of flame
a tiger's eye flash-trace
after harvesters have gathered in the hay

and set the field on fire
still flickers   under the gleam of a sickle moon
from the edge of blackened chaff.

The desert fathers knew
the tricks your mind can play
about absence   pattern   longing   empty space.

Free to Go

Be with me at this window   world of the half-seen.
Everything still   like a hung valley after a gunshot
or my mind   numb   for months after her death.
The wind has dropped. Angles of shutter and floor
are opening out   we are sideways on
to everything we knew   scumbling along as normal
with everything changed   silence buzzing in our ears.

Objects we have chosen to live our lives among
a painting   a stripey rug (or is it a flight
of stairs to a half-landing?)   brown
as the beech-woods she used to play in as a child
     are nearly out of sight
but the world is full of light   and the Andalusian glass
usually its own translucent turquoise   suddenly wild
with roses and the slant ink of their stalks.

Pink! Never her colour. But she'd allow it in a rose.
A good pink she'd say   as long as it smelled good too.
The open window is an exit wound
(she was always there   at the end of a phone)
     joining *outside* to *in*
and her presence   now   the oval of soft grass
where a hare was sleeping a moment ago.

Yellow plums scatter on the table. Dark will come
but we can celebrate   as she would   this gold light
on fresh-picked flowers   and a green-blue vase
answered by the distant sea's blue-green.
     And the body nowhere   free to go   into the air

between   flushed petals and a wash of rose
on the shutter   the street below   gauze cloud
and the Bay of Angels dazzle of indigo.

The Chimborazo Hillstar

For a week I saw no sky. The full moon
was a permanent fixture
above a city black as crêpe

where I lost myself in the swirl
of a one-way system
but each new morning she was still alive

I entered a dim maze of corridors
and found the blue floor arrows
only route I knew to where she lay.

Sometimes her eyes were closed.
Sometimes I found her forcing herself to sip
a beaker of tea. She hated tea but the coffee was worse.

We were on a planet of glass
about to shatter but we laughed
I read her *Emma*

she told the Bulgarian nurse
who kept urging her to eat
    as if food mattered now

that she preferred clear light
to sweet talk of pretence
and spoke of how she'd loved the Zoo.

The science   the romance
of a wilderness within the city
exquisite   endangered animals and plants

like *vulpes zerda*
little bat-eared fennec fox
of the *Moonlight World*

staking his territory
across a miniature
Sahara of white sand.

She knew she was dying.
The caves and valleys
of her defences seemed to change

and her determination
faced with a moonlight world
of emboli and bedpans

the morphine patch she insisted didn't work
the aneurysm that might burst at any moment
reminded me of Chimborazo hillstar

highest-breeding hummingbird
still hanging on
up to the snowline of the Eastern Cordillera

and in the ravines
even in the caves
of golden Cotopaxi   Ecuador.

Set in Gold

This is death   late
       gentlest it could
          she was ninety-seven
               shatterproof

her last word
       after *Where am I?*
          when we said we were all
                    all here with her

was   encouraging us   *Great*
    and Pluto took her
       lord of the underworld
          only god sworn to tell the truth.

Salon Noir

When we went down into the cave
this summer   after her death
had opened the vein to a year of reckoning
across the whole family   everyone upset

     both of them dead within six hours on the same night
     a hundred miles apart   my mother and my aunt
     her sister-in-law
     our gentle   daring   painter
     whose children were rushing her in an ambulance
        from the room upstairs
        in the family house
        where I was born
     to a London hospital
     just when for us it was all over

we were each a little afraid.
Also unprepared. The young   apparently
were thinking of vampires. For me
it was breaking an ankle.

     *

Take nothing   said the guide   a girl
from the green hills of the Ariège
who knew every centimetre of the caves.

Leave behind
all bags and mobile phones.
You're not allowed to take pictures

and you'll need your hands.
The path is slippery
broken   rough

you have to crouch
you'll be carrying a heavy torch
but don't touch the walls

if you stumble. Even your breath
each in-and-out of oxygen
does a little destroying.

    *

Our flashlights in the tunnel   showed
dangerous ridges underfoot.
Wild knobs of embryonic stalagmites
glistened like sea anemones. Beware
they said to our stout shoes   we have time
we *are* time   the texture itself.

The floor of the first
chamber swirled
   like quivers in the structure of a raga.
We were treading limestone waves
millennia of solid flood
breathing shallow as we could

then dark-blistered stone
and pure
     geological process

personal
inexorable
    closed in.

The walls swirled too   when I stopped
to play a beam on them in the dark.
Rough surfaces   map-shapes
of amber   russet   grey
and all around us   black.
No ceramics   no shards

of biscuity pottery
we might piece together into a cup
touched by their lips
fifteen thousand years ago.
This was origin. Way before any potter.
So many ways to begin.

I heard the hiss of time   like the swish of tyres
    on a wet road
as we faltered along   bowed our heads
felt the blowing of solar winds
and the need for fire
like the start cry of a race.

We slipped down a chimney of slime
a tunnel opened out to the *Salon Noir*
and we saw the first human trace
red stripes and black   vertical signs
like sleep-marks on skin
a key-shape   an arrow

we turned off our heavy torches
and laid them down in violet night on a bridge of rock
so our guide could shine her power lamp
of snowy halogen   alone
and we saw bison   flickering the black
circles of their eyes

rippling on cream
stone as if over a canvas of the mind.
I thought of Freud   how the unconscious
is constructed geologically by pressure   a kind
of archaeological layering under the soul
inaccessible except in dreams.

Horses appeared   the tissue of their manes   clear
against grey rock   every tuft erect
scribble-shaggy   bolshie   necks
stretched out   eyes closed   mealy-muzzled as an Exmoor
pony   a whole wall of horses on prehistoric limestone
like a page of Leonardo's sketch-book

whoever drew them had no idea
they would come to be our partners   change
     human work   ambition   history
but I felt at home. Here were the horses
my mum used to draw   for me
     till I could draw my own.

In that milk-flower ray of fluorine
these beasts   called down to the dark
from valleys above   seemed to move

as they must have done then
    for the very first time
in a pitch-flare held for the artist.

While we took it all in   the delicate expressions
the questioning back-turned nose of an ibex
the flaring nostril and lifted tail

of one bison challenging another
I felt my mother's greatest gift
to me was noticing.

She taught us to be curious   to wonder
at all animal life   however small
the territory fights of a chaffinch

fox cubs creeping out at night
their skirmishes with cats.
Snails   she murmured once

at a TV programme on invertebrates.
Who would have thought a snail
could be so tender?

        *

The guide asked if anyone would sing.
The *Salon Noir*   she said   is only one
of many caves. We wonder
if the artists   over the centuries   chose
this chamber for the acoustic   resonant
as a cathedral. Try. I wondered if an echo

might set off an avalanche
and the whole cave-system   the cracked
mysterious mass of hollow stone
would crash   bury us under the mountain
but the notes when they came in that black air
were a flow of prayer   a thread

of unearthly melody like the deep-space vibrato
of a theremin   surely not from my throat.
Our guide followed my song upward with her torch
    a wing-bone of white light   floating into tiered
    pinnacles and funnels of jagged stone
as if lifting us on feathers of pure sound

to the point where all sound disappeared.
I imagined the voice of Orpheus
his aria to life and hope
    ringing out in the kingdom of the dead.
Here in deep earth   the black
blossom of mourning still sifting within me

I remembered that emerald was my birthstone
that an emerald
    mined in the dark
    but lucent green
    as leaves   returning
    after a hundred thousand years of ice

    green for awakening   for bringing life
    back from the dead   renewal
    in earth and of the earth
is a token of re-birth.
I pictured the attic room where I was born
in that enchanted house none of us will enter again

where my mother gave birth to me in May
        her first of five
six if you count the baby that died. I heard
a trickle of water over rock like buried tears
and in this cave of making
        birth of transformation and of art   I understood

how anyone in darkness longs for green
    for the animal life which goes with green
and which   like faceted crystal
      light in stone   lets us see the impossible
      our own lives with their faults and wounds
in a different way

    and how the very idea of one gem for our birth
might make us try
      to say the story of ourselves with a whole heart

    to carry the true good burden of being known
even by animal eyes   and not alone
  like the singer   who drew
all life towards him and went down into the dark
      taking his art into the earth
and art takes him up to the light again   renewed.

We came back changed. We saw black rock
jagged round the entrance   the golden eye
of afternoon. Those who came before
      the dancers   the mothers   were gone into the hill.
But the mountains   rising one behind the other
were herds of green bison   drifting away into the sky.

Notes

THE EMERALD TABLET: is dedicated to Alberto Manguel and Craig Stephenson. The Emerald Tablet itself is the founding text of medieval alchemy. The earliest manuscript is in Arabic, written around the seventh century AD. It was translated into Latin in the twelfth century. (In the seventeenth century, Isaac Newton did a translation into English.) It begins, 'Above is the same as below'.

YOUR LIFE AS A WAVE: Trapiche emeralds have a radial carbon pattern like the wheel of a *trapiche*, a Colombian sugar-cane grinder.

QUANTUM LINKED: The first verse of this poem takes off from the poem *Meaning* by Czesław Miłosz, and a poem I wrote in response to it for Modern Poetry in Translation: *A Salt Wind: Cross Currents in British and Polish Poetry.*

FRAGILE AS BREATH: is dedicated to Ruth Epstein, John Rubin and the Voice Department of the Ear Nose and Throat Hospital, London, with thanks for rescuing my voice.

TUNING YOUR LYRE AMONG THE SHADES, CARBON LABYRINTH, ABOVE IS THE SAME AS BELOW: Ever since the sixteenth century, the world's finest emeralds have been mined in the Eastern Andes, in Colombia. The largest and most enduring mine is at Muzo, above the Minera River in the Emerald Zone of the Boyacá Department, among bright green mountains of rainforest and sugar cane.

FREE TO GO: Matisse painted *Safrano Roses at the Window* (1925) at Nice, looking out on the Bay of Angels.

THE CHIMBORAZO HILLSTAR: This hillstar is a humming-bird endemic to the Ecuadorian volcano Cotopaxi. I found out about it after reading the poem 'Romance', by W. J. Turner, at my mum's funeral. This poem, which she loved as a child, mentions two Ecuadorian volcanoes, Cotopaxi and Chimborazo. I have no idea why a bird that lives on one is called by the name of the other.

SALON NOIR: the Salon Noir is a painted chamber in the pre-historic caves of Niaux, in the Ariège region of the Pyrenees. The theremin is a musical instrument which produces sound without being touched.

Acknowledgements

Warm gratitude, as always, to Parisa Ebrahimi for her dedicated and helpful editorial work; and to Charlotte Humphery at Chatto. Also for perceptive comments to Daphne Astor, Gwen Burnyeat, Aamer Hussein, Alberto Manguel and Declan Ryan.

Thanks to Gwen for bringing me to Colombia, and Andrei Gomez-Suarez and Samuel Gomez for accompanying us to the Emerald Market, Bogota. In India, thanks to Jaisal Singh and Siddharth Kasliwal of the Kasliwal family of Gem Palace, Jaipur, crown jewellers to three generations of emperors; and Nawabzada and Begum Aimaduddin Ahmad Khan, Loharu House, Jaipur, who directed me to the Old Bazaar to talk to an emerald dealer.

Many thanks to Vijay Seshadri and Suzanne Khuri in whose apartment some of these poems began, for their generous and sympathetic hospitality; and to Edward Fitzgerald and Rebecca Fraser for inviting me to the Ariège, and their hospitality there.

Thanks for commissions to Maggie Fergusson and *Intelligent Life* (*The Economist*) which started me off on emeralds; Kaiwan Mehta, the Institut für Auslandsbeziehungen Stuttgart and their 2017 exhibition 'A World in the City: Zoological and Botanic Gardens'; Hannah Crawforth and Elizabeth Scott-Beaumont for commissioning a poem in response to Shakespeare's Sonnet 31, and *RA Magazine* for commissioning one in response to the Royal Academy's 2017 exhibition *Matisse in his Studio*. Also to Sasha Dugdale, *Modern Poetry in Translation* and the Polish Cultural Institute of London, for requesting poems in response to Polish poets.

Thanks to editors of magazines and anthologies where some of these poems first appeared: *Aeon Magazine*; *Compass*

Magazine; Forward Prize *Best Poems 2015*; *here/there poetry*; *The Huffington Post*; *Indian Quarterly*; *Intelligent Life (The Economist)*; *Irish Pages*; *Kenyon Review*; *New Statesman*; *On Shakespeare's Sonnets: A Poets' Celebration* (eds. H. Crawforth and E. Scott-Beaumont, Bloomsbury, 2016); *Plume*; *Poetry London*; *Poetry Review*; *Prac Crit*; *RA Magazine*; *The Spectator*; *Standpoint*; *The White Review*.